D0198545

THE SCIENCE OF.

CREATING CHOCOLATE

by
CLINT TWIST
Consultant
KEITH FARRER

ticktock
MEDIA

CONTENTS

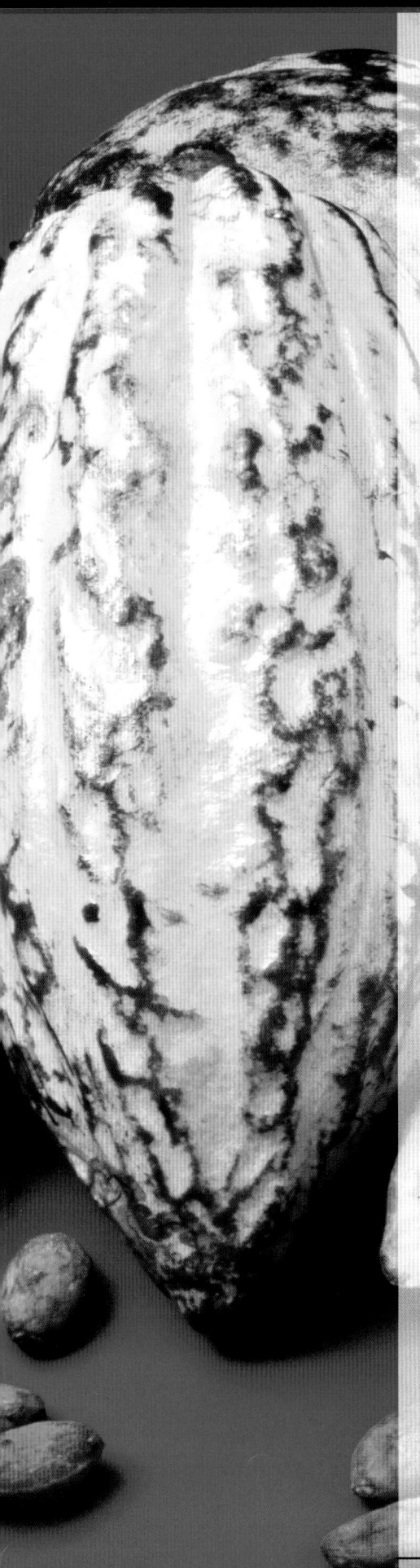

Introduction   **4**

The Best Chocolate Ever   **6**

Safety and Storage   **8**

Getting the Flavour   **10**

Substitute Foods   **12**

Boosting Foods   **14**

Better Ingredients   **16**

Vegetable Meat   **18**

A Whole Meal   **20**

Case Study - A New Soft Drink   **22**

Case Study - Cutting Edge Chips   **24**

Case Study - Tasty Snacks   **26**

Case Study - A Completely New Food   **28**

Glossary   **30**

Index   **32**

Food technologists usually work behind the scenes, and barely known outside the food industry. Although their profession might seem mysterious, we are all familiar with the results of their work. In fact, the chances are that you experienced some of their work when you ate your last meal.

WHAT IS FOOD TECHNOLOGY?

Food technologists aim to improve the food we eat through careful and scientific control of the ingredients. They improve the food we eat and make it: safer, better tasting, healthier, more useful, longer lasting, and more exciting. Food technologists are constantly searching for new and better foods and processes. Sometimes they even invent new foods such as **mycoprotein**, which is now widely eaten as a meat substitute (see page 28).

SCIENTISTS OR CHEFS?

Some food technologists might easily be mistaken for chefs, because they spend all their time in kitchens, devising the best way of preparing a readymade meal that will be produced by the tens of thousands. To do this, they need to understand exactly how each of the ingredients of the meal will be affected by cooking, freezing, and then reheating. Other food technologists seem more like mechanics because their task is to design and maintain the

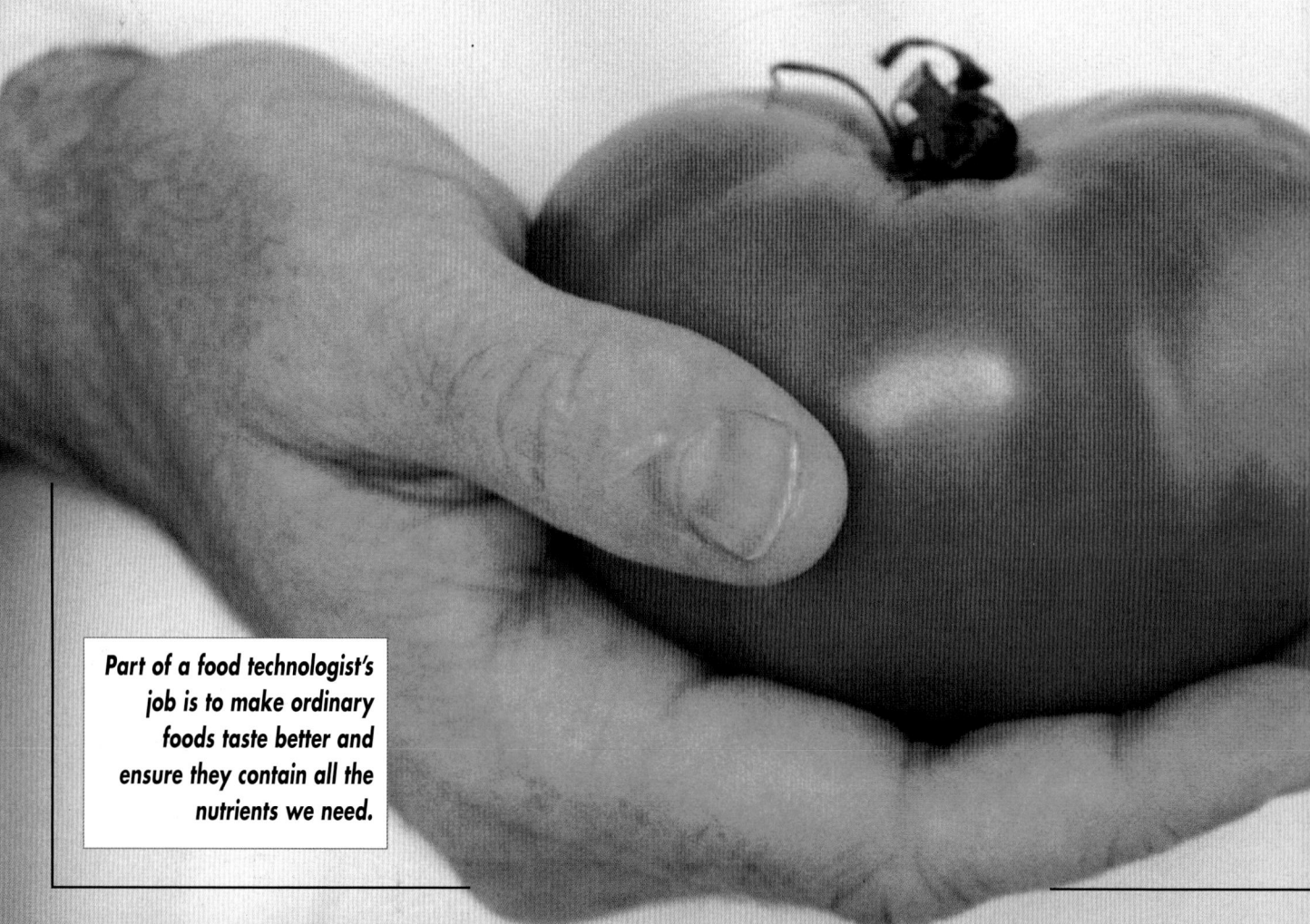

Part of a food technologist's job is to make ordinary foods taste better and ensure they contain all the nutrients we need.

Food scientists spend hours in the laboratory creating exciting new flavours to stimulate the tastebuds of consumers.

machines that are now used to prepare much of our food. Some of these machines operate in surprising ways. Potatoes, for example, are often peeled by high-temperature steam and then cut into chips by a high-speed water gun knife. As well as making our food healthier, food technologists also work hard to make it more fun. They know how to make the smoothest chocolate; how to put the right amount of fizz into a new soft drink; and how to give a crispy snack extra crunchiness. Some of the most important food technologists are the flavour experts, who may never actually see any food during their working day. They spend all their time in the laboratory, mixing tiny amounts of colourless chemicals while trying to find new ways of making old flavours.

KEEPING US HEALTHY

Many food technologists seem more like health workers than cooks or mechanics. They work hard to make sure that our food contains all the **vitamins** and **minerals** we need in order to stay healthy. They also help those people who, for various reasons, cannot eat certain food ingredients. By using their scientific knowledge, technologists can produce milk for people who cannot drink milk (**lactose**-intolerant), and sweet foods for people who cannot eat sugar (**diabetics**).

This food scientist is preparing fruit that will end up in yoghurts, adding preservatives to make it last longer.

Chocolate is made from the ripe seeds of the cacao tree which grows in the tropics. But if you ate one of these seeds it would actually taste quite unpleasant. It takes a considerable amount of technology to turn these seeds – which are confusingly known as cocoa beans – into one of our favourite foods.

FROM THE TREE

After picking, cocoa beans are left piled in the sun for several days. During this time the beans begin to ferment naturally. **Fermentation** is a process in which sugars are broken down into **carbon dioxide** gas and other chemicals. The process is widely used in the food industry — to make bread rise, for example, or to produce alcohol. With cocoa beans, the fermentation allows certain flavour-producing chemicals to develop. The beans are then sent to a factory where they are roasted and then ground into a powder. Most of the natural oil, which is known as cocoa butter, is extracted during the grinding process. What remains is known as chocolate mass — a dark, bitter substance that is the basis for all natural chocolate flavour.

WORKING THE MASS

Some of the chocolate mass will be dried and ground up to produce cocoa powder for use in hot drinks and as a cookery ingredient. In order to make confectionary chocolate, food technologists warm the chocolate mass so that it melts, and add sugar and more oil (usually in the form of cocoa butter). For milk chocolate,

The many different ingredients in this exotic chocolate bar and held together by lecithin.

SCIENCE CONCEPTS

A GOOD MIX

Lecithin (below), which is made from soybeans, is one of a range of food ingredients that are known as emulsifiers. These substances help oils break up into small droplets and mix with other liquids to form an emulsion. Emulsifiers are widely used in the food industry. They also prevent the oil droplets from joining up again causing the oil to separate from the mixture.

JEUNE
LECITHIN
EACH CAPSULE CONTAINS
LECITHIN 1000MG

These Ecuadorian cocoa pods are bursting with ripe beans, which will eventually be turned into delicious chocolate.

either fresh, dried, or condensed milk is added. A substance called lecithin is then added to help the ingredients blend together (*see Science Concepts*). The final part of the process is called conching. Machines beat the mixture vigorously for up to three days, so that the final product has a smooth texture when it cools and solidifies. This is very important because one of the great things about chocolate is that it has excellent "mouthfeel" as well as a delicious flavour.

FINAL TOUCHES

After conching, other ingredients such as fruit, nuts, or pieces of honeycombed sugar may be added to the mix before it is poured into moulds to cool. Chocolate bars that contain two or more different types of chocolate are made by pouring them into the moulds one at a time.

SCIENCE SNAPSHOT

Part of chocolate's wonderful "mouthfeel" is a matter of simple physics. The melting point of chocolate is about the same temperature as the human body (39C). A piece of chocolate that is solid at room temperature begins to melt as soon as you pop it into your mouth, or even if you hold it in your hands for too long.

Food goes bad if it is left for too long before being eaten. This can happen very quickly if the natural packaging is removed, for example by peeling fruit and vegetables. Bad food usually tastes unpleasant and it can cause serious illness. Food **technologists** have developed several ways of making foods more useful by making it last longer.

HOW FOOD GOES BAD

Some foods, such as meat, fresh fruit, and vegetables can be spoiled by contact with the air. The food reacts with the **oxygen** gas in the air and begins to change colour, as when a slice of apple or potato turns brown. This process is known as **oxidation**, and the same thing happens when iron turns to rust. The oxidization of food is not particularly dangerous, but it makes food look very unpleasant.

DANGEROUS PRODUCTS

A much more serious problem is that food is a very good place for microbes, such as **bacteria** and fungi, to live. We are surrounded by

When food is left out in the open for a while, it reacts with oxygen in the air and turns brown.

millions of microbes — in the air and on our skin. Most of them are harmless, but some are very dangerous. They get onto food where they grow and multiply rapidly, and the food begins to decompose and go rotten. Some microbes produce poisonous waste products, and even tiny quantities of these can make a person ill. Keeping food safe from microbes is one of the most important tasks for food technologists.

KEEPING IT SAFE

Proper cooking kills microbes, but this is not much use for preserving food in an uncooked form. Keeping food cool in a refrigerator can slow the growth of microbes, but it does not stop

SCIENCE CONCEPTS

PASTEURISATION

*Fresh milk is made safe for human consumption by a process known as **pasteurisation**. The milk is briefly heated to a temperature of 72C, and then cooled. This kills dangerous microbes, but not those that cause milk to spoil. Fresh milk will start to go bad in a few days even in a refrigerator. Milk that has been heated to 132C is known as UHT milk (ultra-heat-treated) and will keep for several months at room temperature in an opened container.*

them completely. Like all living things, microbes need water, and they cannot grow if they are deprived of water. Food that has been completely dried (dehydrated) can be stored for much longer than fresh food, but not all food is suitable for **dehydration**. Water can also be taken away from microbes by freezing. Because the water is frozen into ice crystals, it is safely locked away from any microbes that may be present. Perhaps the most common way of keeping food fresh for long periods is by canning. Many foods, including meat, fruit, and vegetables, can be kept safe this way. Raw food is sealed inside an airtight metal can and is then heated to kill any microbes. After the can has cooled down, it can be safely stored for several years.

SCIENCE SNAPSHOT

Both freezing and heat treatments such as pasteurisation are necessary to keep our food safe and edible. However, these processes can affect the texture, and even the flavour, of the foods involved. Another way of killing microbes is to use weak doses of nuclear radiation. This process is known as gamma-irradiation. Some scientists do not believe there is not enough evidence to prove this process is completely safe, however, and they also believe that because it changes the chemicals inside the food it has negative effect on the flavour of the food by chemicals inside.

Drying products like coffee means that they can stay fresh and safe to use for many months.

Flavour is the main reason we prefer some foods and drinks to others. Strawberry is a very popular flavour, but not enough strawberries are grown to flavour every product with real strawberries. Some of the most skilled and talented food technologists in the world are employed in creating and blending flavours. The familiar tastes of many of the things we eat and drink were created in the laboratory.

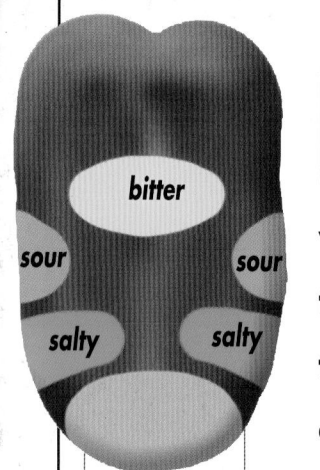

The human tongue has different places for tasting basic flavours.

WHAT IS YUMMY?

Our sense of taste is more complicated than you may think. The taste buds on the tongue can detect only a few basic flavours. These include sweetness, sourness, **saltiness**, and bitterness. Testing something on your outstretched tongue is not really tasting it. The taste buds are a defence mechanism to prevent us from eating poisonous plants, which usually taste very bitter. In order to taste something properly, it has to be inside the mouth where flavour **molecules** can drift up to sense **receptors** in the nose. When we enjoy the flavour of food and drink, we are mainly using our sense of smell. Most substances have a distinctive smell. They release molecules into the air that can be detected by sense receptors. Human beings have a good sense of smell and can recognise thousands of different kinds of smells. Some of these smells are produced by one particular molecule, while others are a combination of many different molecules.

SCIENCE CONCEPTS

FLAVOURING

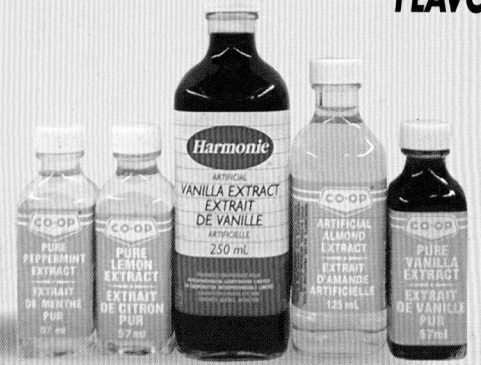

Food flavour is one of those regions of science where the difference between "natural" and "artificial" starts to become meaningless. In some cases the distinction is between two methods of producing the same chemicals. The situation is so complicated that most countries have strict regulations concerning the use of the words "flavour", "flavouring", and "flavoured" on food labelling (see left).

This food researcher is tasting food chemicals on her tongue, and noting down exactly the taste she experiences.

MAKING A FLAVOUR

Popular flavours, such as strawberry, orange, and chocolate, have been analysed and broken down into their different chemical molecules. Once they know exactly what makes a particular flavour, technologists can devise ways of using different ingredients to produce the same effect on the sense receptors.

To make strawberry flavour from ingredients other than strawberries can take more than 300 different ingredients mixed together in exactly the right combination. However, strawberry flavour is easy to make by comparison with the delicious aroma of roasting meat. To produce this flavour in the food laboratory requires nearly 1,000 different ingredients.

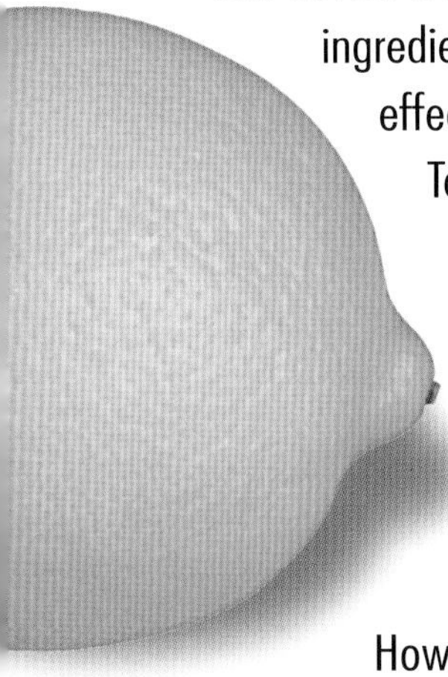

Natural flavours such as orange, lemon and strawberry can now be recreated easily in a laboratory.

✦ SCIENCE SNAPSHOT

The sense receptors in the human nose are very sensitive and can detect some flavour molecules when they are present in concentrations as low as a few in every trillion. When working on a new product, flavour technologists routinely work to an accuracy of one part in one billion.

There are some common food ingredients, such as sugar, milk, and wheat flour that many people cannot eat. This is not a matter or taste or liking. These particular foods can make people feel unwell, and can even make them ill. Food **technologists** must be able to identify these ingredients so that foods can be correctly labelled. They also work hard to produce substitute foods that do not contain these ingredients.

MILK

Everybody can enjoy a drink of milk as a child, but adults in many parts of the world feel unwell if they drink milk. They have a condition known as **lactose** intolerance. This means that their digestive systems cannot tolerate a substance called lactose that is found in all animal milk. So that people with lactose intolerance can enjoy a bowl of breakfast cereal with cold milk, technologists have developed substitute milks made from plant foods which do not contain lactose — for example, soybeans.

> *Carob beans contain natural sugars and are often used as a chocolate substitute.*

SUGAR

Many people suffer from an illness called **diabetes**. People with diabetes (who are known as diabetics) have to be very careful how much sugar they eat. If they have either too much or too little refined sugar, they may become seriously ill. Diabetics have to pay close attention to food labels because many food products contain sugar, even though they do not taste sweet. Technologists have developed a wide range of diabetic food substitutes that have the same taste as ordinary food. For diabetic chocolate, the bitter cocoa mass can be sweetened with fruit sugars, or carob beans may be used instead of cocoa mass.

WHEAT FLOUR

Some people cannot tolerate a substance known as **gluten** which is found in the wheat flour that is the main ingredient of bread, biscuits, and pasta. Smaller quantities of wheat flour are also used in many other food products, for example in sauces.

Gluten is also found in rye flour, but this is not so widely used. Food technologists can help in two ways — either by finding alternative ingredients, or by removing the gluten from flour during the food preparation process. Gluten intolerance often affects infants, and a wide variety of·gluten-free products, including baby-foods, are now available.

> *Soyabeans (right) are grown in North and South America and in China. Special types resistent to herbicides are being grown, which helps the soyabean to thrive.*

SCIENCE CONCEPTS

DANGEROUS ALLERGIES

Peter Pain
PEANUT BUTTER
THEY GO APE OVER IT!

An allergy is when the body has a defence reaction to a particular substance. A common allergy is hay fever, which is caused by the presence of plant pollen in the air. The symptoms of hay fever are usually mild. Some people have allergies to certain foods. In such cases, the body's reaction can be very serious. Over a million Americans have peanut allergy. Their bodies are so sensitive to peanuts that even a small piece of a peanut in a meal will make them seriously ill, and may even kill them. Peanut products are widely used in the food industry, so correct labelling is especially important.

SCIENCE SNAPSHOT

Food technologists are currently working on the peanut allergy problem. They are trying to find out exactly which of the 30 or so unique chemicals in a peanut is responsible for triggering the allergy. When they have identified it, they hope to be able to produce a "safe" peanut that does not contain the problem chemical.

Human beings need to consume small amounts of substances known as **vitamins** and **minerals** in order to remain healthy. This is especially the case for young people and the elderly. These substances are found in fresh foods, but some of them decay during storage, or are destroyed during food preparation. Food technologists add carefully measured doses of vitamins and minerals to some foods, to make sure that everybody stays healthy.

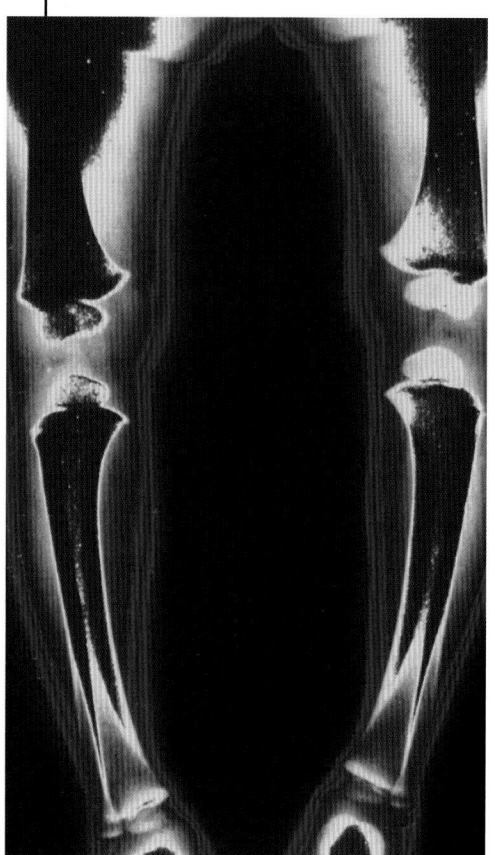

This coloured X-ray shows the bandied legs of a child with rickets, a disease caused by a lack of Vitamin D.

VITAMINS AND MINERALS

Vitamins are chemicals that the body needs for certain tasks, but cannot manufacture for itself. We need different quantities of each vitamin each day. Some of these vitamins are found in lots of foods, while others, such as Vitamin D, are found only in colourful vegetables, deep-sea fish. Minerals are usually chemical elements, such as the metals iron and calcium. The body uses these elements to build useful **molecules**. Iron, for example, is used to make blood **cells**, while calcium is used to make bone.

SCIENCE CONCEPTS

A HEALTHY DIET

There are at least 15 vitamins (scientists are still unsure exactly how many types of vitamin B there are), and another seven vitamin-like substances that are equally important. However, consuming the right amounts of the right vitamins and minerals each day is no guarantee of good health. Nor does it mean that a person is eating a healthy diet (unless all the vitamins and minerals come from fresh food). Food technologists can only help people to health; they cannot make them healthy.

Rice is a good source of magnesium, niacin and vitamin E and B6. However processed rice lacks Vitamin B1, vital for our nerves.

DIET DEFICIENCIES

It is possible to get all the necessary vitamins and minerals by eating a wide range of fresh foods. But this is not always easy, or even possible in some cultures. People who eat a diet consisting mainly of processed rice are liable to develop a disease called beriberi, which affects the nerves. Beriberi is caused by a lack of vitamin B1, and processed rice does not contain this crucial vitamin. People who do not eat enough fresh fruit sometimes develop the disease scurvy, caused by a deficiency of vitamin C. This illness can makes people's teeth fall out, and make them very unwell.

We need vitamins and minerals to keep us healthy and full of energy. Food technicians can now add these to our food.

Technologists often add carefully measured doses of vitamins and minerals to **fortify** popular foods. Breakfast cereals, for example, have been fortified since the 1940s, and since 1998, an American policy of adding **folic acid** to cereal, pasta, bread and flour has resolted in a drop in diseases such as brain and spinal birth defects.

TOO MUCH OF A GOOD THING

The body requires only very small doses of vitamins and minerals. The recommended daily dose for some of them is measured in millionths of a gram. Some vitamins and minerals are poisonous if consumed in larger quantities. People who are very health-conscious and who take vitamins pills, as well as all the vitamins in their food may run the risk of poisoning themselves.

SCIENCE SNAPSHOT

Cholesterol is a type of **fat** that is essential to the workings of the human body. It is found in foods such as meat and dairy products. Many people believe that too much cholesterol in the body can lead to heart disease. Food technologists have discovered a substance that can lower the amount of cholesterol in the human body. This substance is now being added to certain food products, milk for example, so that people can eat it as part of an ordinary meal.

Food scientists can make food more useful by altering the food itself. Traditional methods have already improved many crops (food plants) by increasing their productivity. But the new technology of genetic modification (GM) means that food technologists will be able to create crops that have exactly the characteristics that the technologists want them to have.

GENETIC MODIFICATION

Almost every **cell** in every living thing contains a **molecule** called **DNA**. This molecule is made up of a series of chemically coded instructions that are called genes. Every species has its own particular set of genes (known as its **genome**). But this does not mean that every member of the species is exactly the same - genes vary from individual to individual.

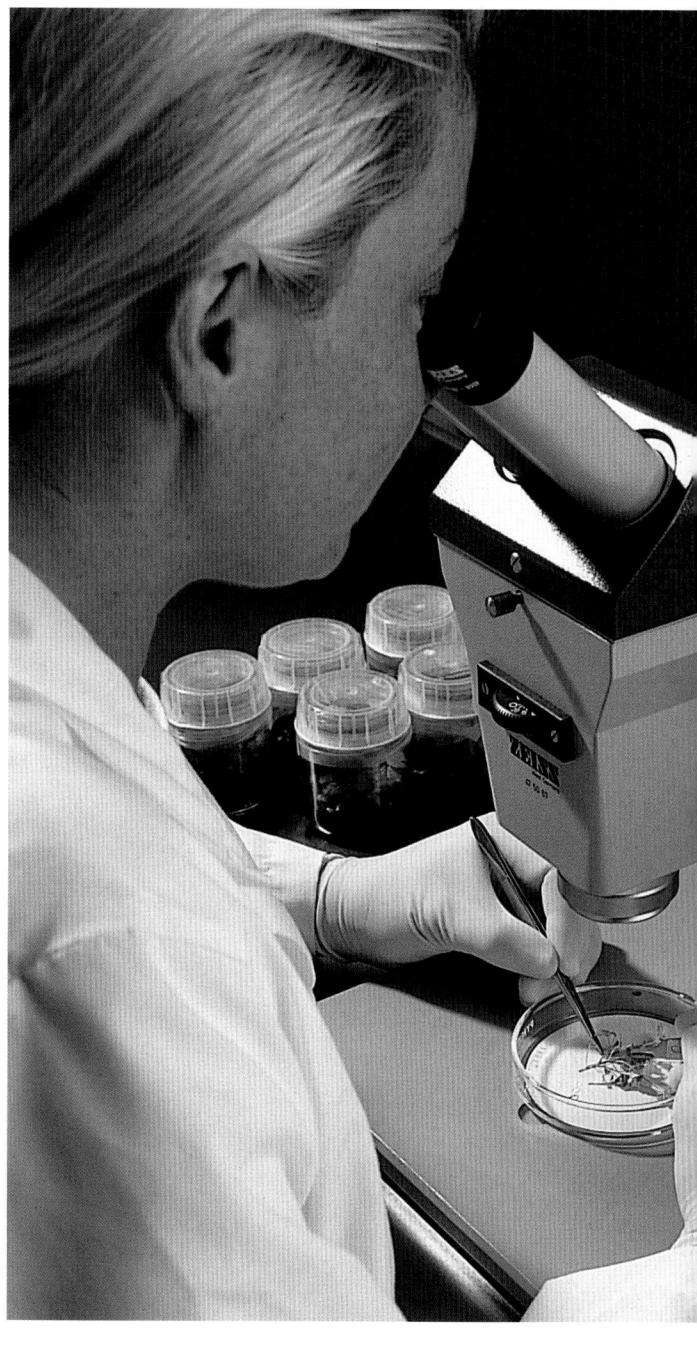

> *This scientist is dissecting pieces of plant matter under a microscope in preparation for gene splicing (see page 17).*

SCIENCE CONCEPTS

GM SAFETY

Laboratory tests have shown that the GM versions of these crops are perfectly safe for humans to eat – but this is not the only concern about their safety. Some scientists believe that the modified genes in these crops can be spread to other plants by pollen blowing on the wind. This would mean that some weeds would soon become resistant to weed killers. Tests are being carried out to find out exactly how far pollen from GM crops can travel. Many groups have protested against GM food by destroying fields containing these crops (left).

An ordinary tomato will decay in a matter of days, but a genetically modified one will last up to an extra 20 days.

Genes decide how tall a person will grow, how good their eyesight is, and whether they will suffer from **lactose** intolerance. Scientists have learnt how to extract DNA from cells and snip out a particular gene. They can then replace it with a different gene and then put the DNA back into the cells. This process is sometimes called **gene splicing**; it is used mainly in medicine and the food industry. Gene splicing will not work on some plants. Instead the modified DNA has to be blasted into seeds on microscopic particles of gold. This technique is known as "shot gunning".

GM FOODS

Technologists have already produced GM versions of some crops — soybeans and oil-seed rape for example. Their genes have been altered to make them resistant to weed killers. Farmers can spray a whole field with weed killer and only the weeds are killed, while the GM crops remain unaffected. This means that the crops can grow bigger, farmers do not waste water on weeds, and harvesting is much easier. GM crops are now grown in some countries, and are used as ingredients in a wide variety of foods. In other countries, however, people are still very concerned about the safety of GM crops. They want all foods with GM ingredients to be very clearly labelled so that people can decide for themselves whether or not they want to eat them.

SCIENCE SNAPSHOT

Tomatoes begin to rot as soon as they are picked, because one of their genes turns on the rotting process. Food technologists have learned how to turn off this gene - by removing it; turning it upside down, and then putting it back in the tomato's DNA. The result is tomatoes that stay fresh on the shelves for much longer than those that have not been modified.

Plant protein can be turned into a variety of different food products, from sandwich fillings to burgers.

Many people choose not to eat meat – they are **vegetarians.** This is usually because they have strong views about killing animals or because their religion forbids them to eat animals. Meat is a natural part of our diet, but it is not essential to our survival. The most difficult part of a vegetarian diet is making sure that you get enough protein. Food **technologists** have helped to make this easier.

PLANT PROTEIN

Meat is a valuable source of **protein**. Using protein extracted from plants, food technologists have been able to create vegetarian meat that smells, tastes, and chews just like real meat. Soybeans are especially suitable for the production of vegetarian meat because they have a fairly high natural protein content of about 50 percent. The beans are processed and the protein is concentrated produce a mixture that is about 70 percent protein. This can be flavoured and treated in a number of different ways to produce different "meat" products. The easiest product to make is vegetarian minced meat. The soy protein is made into stiff paste that breaks up into small pieces called granules. These can be dried and added to recipes instead of minced meat. If the food technologists want the product to have more chewiness, they use a heat process that alters the protein making it chewier. The best quality vegetarian meats use a more complex process. The protein is broken down by chemicals and is then spun into narrow fibres that are thinner than human hairs. These fibres can be knitted or woven (just like textile fibres) to produce foods that have nearly the same texture and mouthfeel (see page 7) as real meat.

SCIENCE CONCEPTS

TYPES OF PROTEIN

Protein is an essential part of our diet, but our bodies do not mind whether it is plant protein or animal protein as long as they get enough protein. Animal protein is much more expensive to produce than vegetable protein, as animals have to fed and cared for until they are old enough to be taken to the slaughterhouse.

Traditional cheeses like the ones on the left contain an animal byproduct called rennet. It traps the fat, which gives the cheese its flavour.

OTHER INGREDIENTS

Cheese made from milk is a valuable source of protein. Many vegetarians allow themselves dairy products such as fresh milk and butter, but they will not eat ordinary cheese. Most cheese making involves the use of a substance called rennet which is extracted from dead cows. The rennet allows the **fats** and protein to be extracted for cheese making. Food technologists have developed a plant-based alternative to rennet, and this is now used to make vegetarian cheese.

SCIENCE SNAPSHOT

Lots of people enjoy the taste of bacon, but it is forbidden to vegetarians and people whose religions do not allow them to eat pork. Food technologists have produced both beef bacon and vegetarian bacon that have the look and taste of the real thing.

Today, many people do not always have the time to cook a traditional meal from fresh ingredients. Food **technologists** make life easier by producing a range of prepared foods, such as readymade sauces that can be served with pasta or rice. Even more convenient is an entire meal that is prepared and pre-cooked. All the busy shopper has to do is take it home and heat it properly in an oven or microwave.

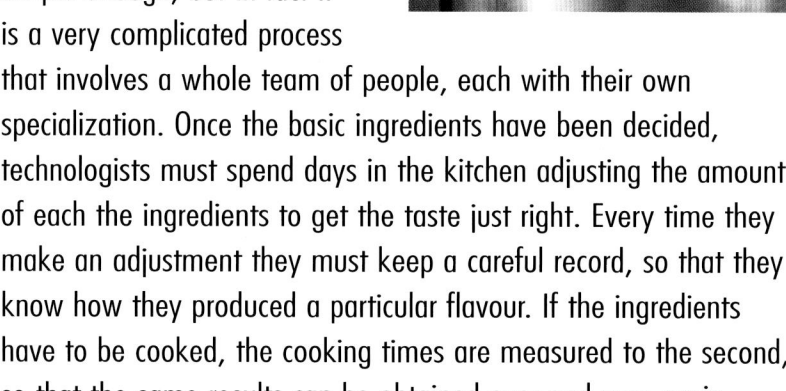

FIVE STAR CHEFS

Creating a readymade meal is a tremendous challenge for food technologists. It sounds simple enough, but in fact it is a very complicated process that involves a whole team of people, each with their own specialization. Once the basic ingredients have been decided, technologists must spend days in the kitchen adjusting the amount of each the ingredients to get the taste just right. Every time they make an adjustment they must keep a careful record, so that they know how they produced a particular flavour. If the ingredients have to be cooked, the cooking times are measured to the second, so that the same results can be obtained over and over again.

MADE TO KEEP

Getting the meal to taste like as though it was made by a restaurant chef is only the first stage because readymade meals are not eaten straight away. Food technologists also have to

Although convenient, ready meals are not always a healthy option as they contain a higher amount of salt and fat.

SCIENCE CONCEPTS

READING THE LABEL

When you buy a readymade meal you are buying two things – the food, and the instructions as to how it should be stored and served. These instructions are not just a suggestion – they have been prepared by food technologists who want you to enjoy your meal. Many readymade meals require heating to a certain temperature for a particular length of time. Always read and follow the instructions on such meals – if they are not heated sufficiently before being eaten, they may cause illness.

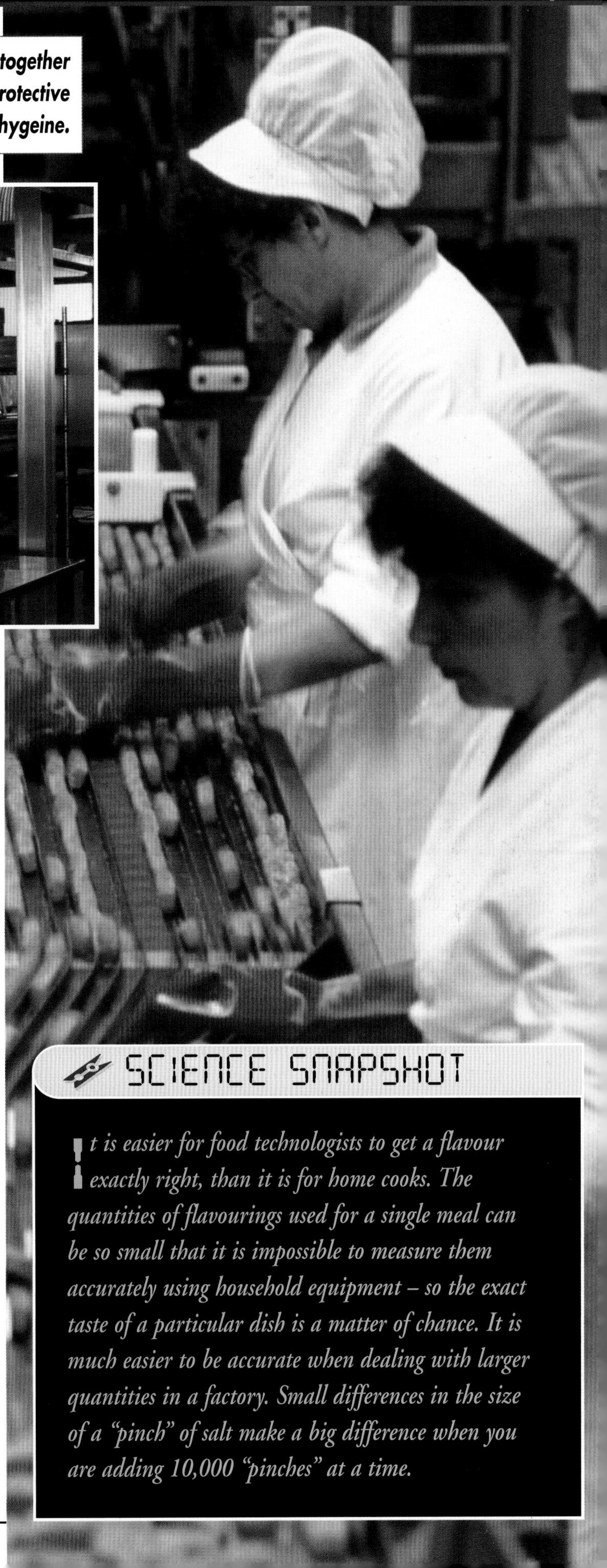

Workers in a food factory work on an assembly line, putting together the different elements of a meal. They must wear hats and protective clothing to maintain the highest level of hygeine.

Ingredients for ready meals are produced in huge quantities.

consider the problems of storage. Such meals are usually sold either frozen or chilled. Samples of each meal must be stored for different lengths of time, and then tested to see whether the flavours of the meal or the quality of the ingredients have been affected. Recipes often have to be further adjusted so that they will store better. When they have produced a meal that tastes good and stores well, the technologists still have a lot of work to do.

MASS MADE

Readymade meals are not made one at a time in a small kitchen. They are prepared and cooked by the thousand in large factories, where most of the workers will never see the completed product (some of the "workers" may even be robots). Food technologists have to devise the most efficient way of producing their meal in large numbers. They also have to ensure that the quality of the ingredients is constantly checked. Only when the first batch of meals leaves the factory is their task completed.

SCIENCE SNAPSHOT

It is easier for food technologists to get a flavour exactly right, than it is for home cooks. The quantities of flavourings used for a single meal can be so small that it is impossible to measure them accurately using household equipment – so the exact taste of a particular dish is a matter of chance. It is much easier to be accurate when dealing with larger quantities in a factory. Small differences in the size of a "pinch" of salt make a big difference when you are adding 10,000 "pinches" at a time.

Soft drinks are big business. Around the world each year people drink billions of cans and bottles of their favourite drinks. Developing a new product – one with an exciting and refreshing taste - can take months, even years of work. Food **technologists** become part of a large team all working toward the same goal.

Researchers can develop improved products by interviewing consumers about their favourite drinks.

RESEARCH AND DEVELOPMENT

Research is the essential first stage of the process. Consumers are interviewed and asked what they like most about their favourite drink, and what they do not like about other drinks. The researchers may also ask about people's attitude to health and fitness. The information obtained from hundreds of interviews is used to decide the basic design of the new drink — what flavour it will have, what colour it will be, whether it will be still or sparkling, and whether it will contain sugar or **artificial sweeteners.** This design is then handed over to the drinks technologists who decide exactly which ingredients to use. They will produce many versions of the drink, each with a slightly different combination of ingredients. These are tested at special testing sessions to see what strength of flavour most people prefer.

ADDING BUBBLES

If the drink is to be sparkling, the tasting sessions will also decide exactly how sparkling should it be. A process known as **carbonation** adds the sparkle to soft drinks. **Carbon dioxide** gas is forced into the drink under **pressure** so that it dissolves in the liquid. The gas will stay in the drink for as long as it is stored under pressure. When the pressure is released (by opening a can or bottle for the first time) the carbon dioxide bubbles out of the liquid. This creates the fizzy sensation in the mouth that many people enjoy. However, carbonation can also affect the flavour of the other ingredients, so the technologists have to be very careful to add exactly the right amount of fizz.

ALWAYS THE SAME

People have a favourite soft drink because that particular drink always tastes exactly the same. They can look forward to quenching their thirst and enjoying that particular set of flavours. Wherever they go, they know that their favourite drink will always taste just the way they like it. The end result of the soft drink development process is not the drink itself, but a detailed list of instructions for making that drink. These instructions are known as the drink's **formula**, and they are very detailed indeed. It is not enough to simply say "water" - the taste of water from different localities varies slightly because it contains naturally occurring **minerals**. A drink's formula usually contains precise instructions for how water is to be treated before it is added to the other ingredients.

When a food researcher tests orange juice, for example, they drink it whilst a nasal sensor detects flavour molecules in the nose.

CASE STUDY FACTFILE

- *Careful research is the first stage of any development project.*
- *When experimenting with different flavours, it is very important to keep an accurate record of which ingredients are used.*
- *Carbonation is the name of the process that makes soft drinks sparkling.*
- *The bubbles in a sparkling drink are an important part of how it tastes.*
- *Each soft drink has its own unique formula – precise instructions as to how to prepare the drink.*

This researcher is monitoring water quality in a drinks factory. The type and quality of water used must be consistent every time the product is tested.

C hips are one of the most popular foods in the world, and millions are eaten every day. Some of these are prepared and cooked by hand using traditional methods, but most are now made by machines in modern factories. Machines are widely used in the food industry because they are reliable and efficient. Some foods, such as chips, can be prepared with hardly any assistance from human workers.

Only large potatoes are turned into chips.

HANDLING

Making chips by hand takes both time and care. Each potato must be washed, peeled, and then carefully cut with a knife - first into slices, and then into chips that are ready for the pan. Inside a factory, machines designed by food technologists use some very unusual methods to achieve exactly the same result. Fresh potatoes are unloaded into large tanks of water that are about the same size as a public swimming pool. Rocks and soil sink to the bottom of the tank, while the potatoes float at the surface. The potatoes are then washed across a series of screens that filter out those that are too small for making chips. Those that make the grade are moved along a series on water channels and onto **conveyor belts**.

PEELING

Removing the skin from a potato with a knife or scraper is complicated and time-consuming. It is much easier to use a bit of simple steam-powered science. As the potatoes move along the conveyor belt they are blasted with high-temperature steam for a few seconds. This causes water in the layer of potato underneath the skin to boil. The boiling water turns to steam and expands very rapidly, and the potato skin is literally blown off by the force of this expansion. The freshly "peeled" potatoes continue along the conveyor, while the skins are collected for animal feed.

CUTTING

When producing chips in large quantities, it is important that each chip has the same width and depth so that they will all cook evenly. Cutting one potato into equally sized chips is hard to do: imagine having to cut thousands and thousands of potatoes each day. Factories that produce chips use one of the most ingenious

Peeled potatoes are sifted by this machine.

machines in the whole of the food industry - the Water Gun Knife. This machine does something that human workers just cannot do. It uses a jet of high-**pressure** water to shoot potatoes through a metal grid at about 130 km/h. The uprights and crosspieces of the grid are razor sharp blades. As the potatoes are blasted through the grid they are cut neatly into chips of the required size.

Water guns like this one can cut chips at a faster rate than any person possibly could.

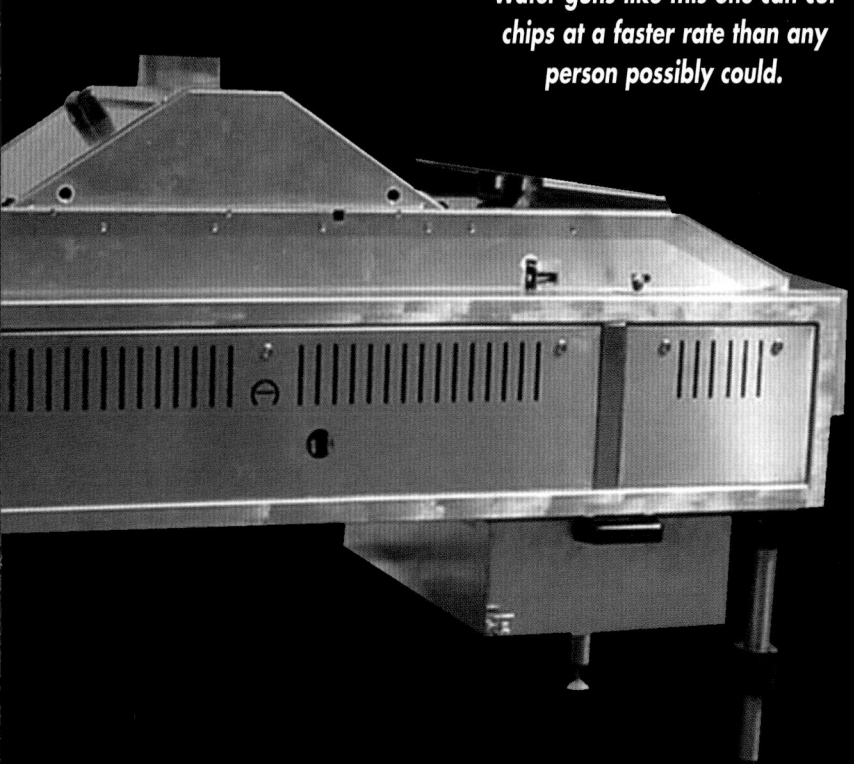

COMPUTER-CONTROLLED

All the machines that are used for sorting, peeling, and cutting potatoes are controlled by computers that keep the conveyor belts moving at the correct speeds. Throughout the process, sensors keep an electronic eye on quality control. These sensors can detect tiny differences in colour, and any imperfect chips are quickly removed from the conveyor belt by mechanical arms. After being cut, the chips are dried by hot air blowers before being cooked in automatic frying machines. They are then cooled and frozen for distribution.

CASE STUDY FACTFILE

- *Today, machines in large, high-speed factories produce most chips.*
- *Inside a factory, potatoes move at speeds up to 130 km/h.*
- *Machines use high-temperature steam to blast off potato skins.*
- *Potatoes are often cut into equally sized chips by a machine called a Water Gun Knife.*
- *Electronic sensors scan the chips before cooking to detect any imperfections.*

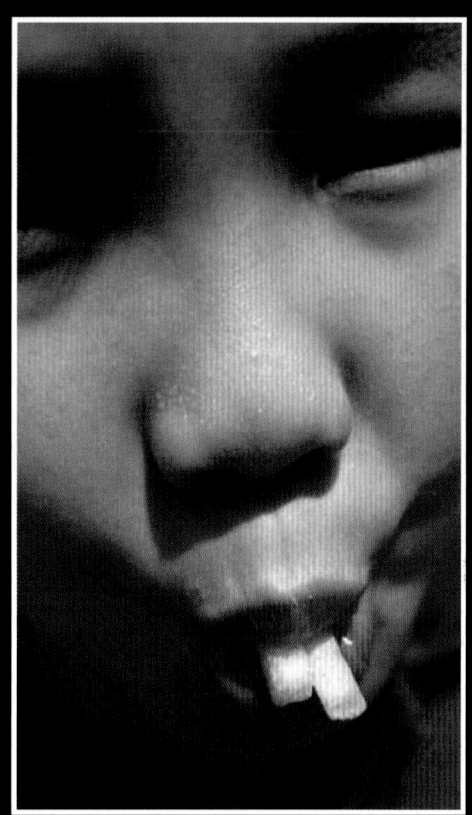

Despite the health risks associated with eating too much fat, chips remain a popular snack.

Crispy and crunchy snacks are a very popular food, especially among young people. A combination of crispiness and strong flavour makes these snacks fun to eat. Food **technologists** work hard to create exciting new flavours and to make their products more and more tasty. One way of doing this is to add more **salt** to the ingredients. But some people believe that crispy snacks already contain too much salt.

SNACK PRODUCTION

The original crispy snacks were potato crisps — very thin slices of potato fried until they are golden brown and crunchy. Some snacks are still made in this way, but the majority of them are not made from sliced vegetables. The main ingredient of most crispy snacks is **flour** — usually potato flour, corn flour, or rice flour. The flour is mixed with water into a thick paste, to which flavourings and other ingredients are added. This paste can then be rolled, pressed, moulded, and squirted into a wide variety of shapes. Air can also be bubbled through the paste to make the final product even crunchier. After cooking, the snacks are often sprinkled with additional flavouring before being packaged.

*Although most people think crisps are made from potatoes, most are now made out of **flour** and water!*

SALT

The word salt usually refers to table salt, which is the popular name for the naturally occurring chemical, sodium chloride. People have been adding salt to their food for thousands of years, and it is the oldest of all food flavourings. Saltiness is one of the basic tastes that can be detected by the tongue, but the main reason it is added to food is that salt makes other flavours taste much better - it is a flavour enhancer. Most recipes in cookery books include a "pinch" of salt among the ingredients, and most prepared foods contain a little salt. Crispy snacks, however, often contain considerably more. Our bodies need a little salt each day in order to remain healthy, but many people eat much more salt than they need. There is evidence that too much salt in the diet may lead to illness in later life. Some health experts have become concerned about the amount of salt that people eat.

A bowl of crisps like these contain a considerable amount of salt, which is not good for us.

CRAMMED WITH FLAVOUR

Most crispy snacks have a strong flavour. Some are flavoured with uncooked ingredients such as cheese, onion, and garlic, some have cooked flavours such as crispy bacon or roast beef, while others have a mainly hot flavour such as chilli. Some snacks have a special flavour formula - a combination of ingredients, some of which may be natural and some laboratory made. Whatever flavourings are used, you can be almost certain that your crispy snack contains salt.

Salt mines like these are actually deposits left behind from evaporated sea water.

Perhaps the most exciting and important work carried out by food technologists is the development of new sources of food. One of these new food sources is **mycoprotein**, which is used as a meat substitute. The great advantage of mycoprotein is that it is not produced on farms where it can be affected by bad weather. Instead it is "grown" inside steel tanks in a factory.

A scientist examines fungus samples in the laboratory. Scientists developing mycoprotein had to work out the best way to produce it in large quantaties.

FROM THE SOIL

Mycoprotein is neither animal nor vegetable - it is made from a tiny, single-celled **fungus** that lives in soil. The fungus, which has a high **protein** content, was discovered in the 1960s after scientists began a worldwide search for alternative sources of protein. Discovering the fungus, however, was just the first step towards a new food. Technologists had to learn how to grow the fungus in a laboratory so that it could be fully tested. When they were sure that mycoprotein was safe to eat, they then had to develop a method of producing it in large quantities. At the same time, other technologists experimented with ways of flavouring the new food. After years of hard work, the commercial production of mycoprotein eventually started in the mid-1980s.

Quorn burgers were launched in 1994, but it was not until 2002 that Quorn was approved for sale in the United States.

NON-STOP PRODUCTION

Mycoprotein is produced by what is known as a continuous-culture system. Like most single-celled organisms, the fungus can be made to grow outside its natural habitat in a mixture of water, sugar, and **mineral**s. This method is known as culturing, and it is mainly used in laboratories to produce very small quantities. Producing large quantities of mycoprotein requires culturing on a large scale in huge stainless steel tanks. Water, sugar and minerals are pumped in at one end of the tank and waste products, mainly **carbon dioxide** gas, are extracted at the other. Under ideal conditions, at about 30C, the amount of fungus doubles every five hours. It is "harvested" continuously by mechanical filters, and is then ready for flavouring and packing.

FOOD PRODUCTS

The individual fungus cells are shaped like tiny threads. This gives mycoprotein a very good basic texture and there is no need to process it into fibres as is sometimes done with soy protein. Food technologists have used their skills to flavour mycoprotein so that it resembles different meats, such as chicken, turkey, ham, and beef. It can be used instead of meat in a wide variety of recipes, and there are also mycoprotein sausages and burgers - there are even mycoprotein cold cuts that can be sliced to make sandwiches. Food products containing mycoprotein have been sold in Europe since the 1980s and they are now available in most parts of the world.

CASE STUDY FACTFILE

- *Mycoprotein is a meat-substitute produced from a single-celled fungus.*
- *It took about 20 years to develop mycoprotein as a commercial source of food.*
- *Mycoprotein is produced by culturing a fungus in a mixture of water, sugar, and minerals.*
- *Under ideal condition the amount of fungus doubles every five hours.*
- *The individual fungus cells, which are shaped like tiny threads, give mycoprotein a good texture.*

Quorn is a brand name used for mycoprotein. It can be flavoured and shaped to imitate various meats.

Allergy - a medical condition in which a person's body has a very strong reaction to an otherwise harmless substance, such as dust, pet hair, or peanuts.

Artificial sweetener – a chemical substance that is used instead of sugar to hide bitterness and sourness, or to make food and drink taste sweet.

Bacteria – single-celled organisms that are found in every environment from the bottom of the sea to inside our bodies. Most bacteria are harmless; some cause our food to go bad, while a few can cause disease.

Carbonation – the process of forcing carbon dioxide gas into a liquid under pressure. When the pressure is released the gas bubbles out of the liquid, making it fizzy.

Carbon dioxide – a colourless and odourless gas that is naturally present in the air in small quantities.

Cells The 'building-blocks' of living things. The smallest unit of an organism

Conveyor belt – a continuous loop of fabric, plastic, or rubber that moves over a series of rollers to form a continually moving surface on which objects can be transported from one place to another.

Dehydration – the process of removing all of the water from a particular substance that normally contains water.

Diabetes – the popular name for diabetes mellitus, a disease that affects the body's ability to process sugar.

DNA – abbreviation that stands for deoxyribonucleic acid, a molecule found in the cells of most living things, that carries coded information in the form of genes.

Emulsion – a mixture of two liquids, in which one of the liquids is in the form of tiny droplets spread evenly throughout the other liquid.

Fat – one of the main constituents of food (along with protein and carbohydrate). Fat is plant or animal tissue that contains a lot of oil.

Fermentation – the process by which molecules of sugar are broken down to form other substances, such as alcohol, and carbon dioxide is produced as a waste product.

Flour – a powdery substance made by drying and grinding the seeds or roots of some plants. Used by itself, the word flour usually refers to wheat flour.

Folic acid – A vitamin essential for cell growth and reproduction.

Formula – the precise instructions, including a detailed list of ingredients, for making a particular substance.

Fungus – a type of organism that is neither plant nor animal. A fungus grows somewhat like a plant, but does not make use of sunlight. Mushrooms, moulds, and yeasts are the most common kinds of fungus.

Gamma irradiation – The use of radiation for the sterilization or preservation of food.

Gene – a set of coded instructions in a molecule of DNA that affects one particular characteristic of an organism, such as eye colour or the ability to process lactose.

Genome – An organism's genetic material.

Gene splicing – a method of inserting a gene into a DNA molecule.

Gluten – A mixture of insoluble plant proteins occurring in cereal grains, chiefly corn and wheat. Used to make dough sticky.

GM – abbreviation of "genetically modified", which describes any organism that has had one or more of its genes artificially altered by scientists and technologists.

Lactose – a form of sugar that is naturally present in milk. Most people lose the ability to process lactose when they become adult.

Magnesium – Ssilver-white light metallic element that occurs in bones for example.

Mineral – in food technology, the word mineral usually refers to one of the chemical elements, such as iron or sodium, which the body requires in very small quantities.

Molecule – the smallest chemical unit of a particular substance, composed of one or more atoms. A molecule of carbon dioxide, for example, contains one atom of carbon and two atoms of oxygen.

Mycoprotein – an edible protein that is obtained from a fungus.

Niacin – An acid present in meat, wheat germ, and dairy products.

Oxidation – the process by which many substances are changed when they come into contact with oxygen as, for example, when iron turns to rust.

Oxygen – a colourless and odourless gas that is naturally present in the atmosphere. When we breathe, our bodies convert some of the oxygen to carbon dioxide.

Pasteurisation – a heat treatment for milk and other liquids that is named for the French scientist Louis Pasteur who discovered the process. Pasteurisation kills harmful microbes, but not those that cause milk to go bad.

Pressure – the physical force of one object against another when the two are in contact. When you blow up a balloon, you fill it with gas that is at a higher pressure than that of the surrounding air.

Protein – one of the main constituents of food (along with fat and carbohydrate). The body uses protein molecules to build new cells and repair old ones.

Receptors – the nerve cells that line the internal passages of the nose and detect flavour molecules.

Salt – by itself, the word salt usually refers to table salt, the chemical sodium chloride. In chemistry there are many different salts, of which sodium chloride is just one.

Sodium chloride – the chemical name for table salt.

Technologist – Someone who uses scientific knowledge to solve practical problems

UHT – abbreviation of ultra-heat treated, the process of heating food above 100C to kill all microbes, so that it can be stored for long periods.

Vegetarian – describes a person who does not eat meat, a restaurant that does not serve meat, or a product that does not contain meat in any form.

Vitamin – a chemical substance that is essential for good health and that is found in one or more types of fresh food.

A

allergies, *see food intolerances*

artificial sweeteners 22, 30

B

bacteria 30

beriberi 15

C

carbon dioxide 6, 23, 29, 30

carbonation, *see carbon dioxide*

carob beans 12

cereals 15

cheese 19

chips 24–25

chocolate 5, 6–7, 12

cholesterol 15

crisps 26–27

D

dehydration 9, 30

diabetes 12, 30

DNA 16–17, 30

dried foods 9

E

emulsifiers 6, 30

emulsion, *see emulsifiers*

F

fermentation 6, 30

fats 19, 30

flavour 5, 10–11, 21, 22, 23

food allergies, *see food intolerances*

food intolerances 5, 12–13, 30

food poisoning 8

food scientists, *see food technologists*

food technologists 4, 5, 8, 11, 12, 13, 14, 15, 16, 17, 18, 20–21, 22, 23, 24, 25, 28–29

frozen food 9

fruit 10, 11, 15

G

gamma-irradiation 9

genes 16–17, 30

gene splicing 17, 30

genomes 16

genetic modification (GM) 16, 17, 30

GM foods 17

gluten 12

gluten intolerance, *see gluten and food intolerances*

H

health 4, 5, 14, 15, 27

L

lactose 12, 30

lecithin 6–7

M

meat 18, 19

microbes 8, 9

milk 5, 8, 12, 15

minerals 5, 14, 15, 23, 28, 30

molecules 10, 14, 31

mycoprotein 4, 28, 29, 30

N

nuclear radiation, *see gamma-irradiation*

O

oxidation 8, 30

P

pasteurisation 8, 9

peanuts 13

pesticides, *see weed-killers*

protein 18, 19, 28, 30

Q

quorn, *see mycoprotein*

R

readymade meals 4, 20

receptors, *see sense receptors*

rennet 19

rickets 14

rotting food 8–9, 17

S

salt 10, 26–27, 30

scurvy 15

sense receptors 10–11, 30

soft drinks 22–23

soya beans 6, 12–13, 17, 18

sugar 5, 12, 29

T

taste buds, *see taste*

taste 4, 10, 20, 26–27

V

vegetarianism 4, 18–19, 30

vitamins 5, 14, 15, 30

W

weed-killers 16, 17

Copyright © ticktock Entertainment Ltd 2004

First published in Great Britain in 2004 by ticktock Media Ltd.,

Unit 2, Orchard Business Centre, North Farm Road, Tunbridge Wells, Kent, TN2 3XF

We would like to thank: Elizabeth Wiggans and Jenni Rainford for their help with this book.

ISBN 1 86007 594 0 HB   ISBN 1 86007 588 6 PB

Printed in China

A CIP catalogue record for this book is available from the British Library.

Picture Credits

Alamy: 2-3 and 7t, 4-5, 8t, 20l, 25br, 26l, 26-27tc, 27br. Anthony Blake: 12c, 14b, 20-21 t, 21r, 24l, 25t, 25b, 28-29ct, 29br. Corbis: 5 all, 6b, 8b, 10-11 centre, 14-15c, 15t, 16c. Science Photo Library: 9b, 11r, 14l, 17r, 22-23c, 23r, 28c, Still Pictures: 16b.